Emotional Intelligence

Why it is Crucial for Success in Life and Business

7 Simple Ways to Raise Your EQ, Make Friends with Your Emotions, and Improve Your Relationships

PUBLISHED BY: James W. Williams

Copyright © 2019 All rights reserved.

No part of this publication may be copied, reproduced in any format, by any means, electronic or otherwise, without prior consent from the copyright owner and publisher of this book.

Table of Contents

Your Free Gift 4

Introduction 6

Chapter 1 11

What is Emotional Intelligence 11

Chapter 2 17

The Benefits of Emotional Intelligence 17

Chapter 3 25

Raising Your Emotional Intelligence 25

Closure 39

Thank you! 43

Your Free Gift

As a way of saying thanks for your purchase, I wanted to offer you a free bonus E-book called **Bulletproof Confidence Checklist** exclusive to the readers of this book.
To get instant access just tap here, or go to:
https://theartofmastery.com/confidence/

Inside the book, you will discover:
- What is shyness & social anxiety, and the psychology behind it
- Simple yet powerful strategies for overcoming social anxiety
- Breakdown of the traits of what makes a confident person
- Traits you must DESTROY if you want to become confident

- Easy techniques you can implement TODAY to keep the conversation flowing
- Confidence checklist to ensure you're on the right path of self-development

Introduction

Emotional intelligence is extremely important and is critical for success both in personal and professional life. It helps you develop leadership skills, maintain meaningful relationships, and navigate skillfully through difficult periods of life. So, how much effort you put into developing or improving your emotional intelligence depends partly on how much you care about the quality of your relationships, and partly on how far you want to get professionally.

Emotional intelligence has become one of the most sought-after skills in the workplace, mainly because employers are increasingly looking for people who are good team-players, who work well under pressure, and who can communicate effectively in a culturally diverse environment.

Emotional intelligence can help you develop and

perfect these skills by sensitizing you both to your own emotions and to those of others, and by encouraging you to constantly work on improving your relationships.

While some people are natural empaths, for most of us it's a learned skill. Those who are used to analyzing their emotions are probably also good at understanding the emotions and motives of others. In which case, they'll find it easy to develop emotional intelligence.

Unfortunately, most people are too self-centered and concerned only with their own problems and life and are simply not interested in others. Most would rather give a donation than become actively involved in helping someone, even if only to spend some time listening to them. Although this is partly due to the busy and stressful lives most of us live, it's also because our culture has only recently recognized the importance of emotional intelligence for one's wellbeing and the reasons many people struggle to develop it.

So, emotional intelligence revolves around empathy, and the ability to understand and manage your emotions. Managing emotions is about understanding the trigger that had caused a particular emotion, and not responding to the trigger until you've had time to fully understand what you are feeling and why. And when you can manage your emotions, you can manage any situation you find yourself in.

This gives you the edge over others because you are not only able to resolve a conflict before it gets out of hand, but because you know how to recognize and avoid situations which may lead to a conflict.

If, as part of your job or lifestyle, you often have to deal with a great number of people, you are probably well aware of how important interpersonal relationships are, and how good communication, or lack of it, can facilitate or complicate things.

We all have relationship problems from time to time, and what is particularly annoying is realizing, with hindsight, that many of them could have been avoided had the communication been better. This is one of the reasons why emotional intelligence is such an important skill in the workplace.

People who are in touch with their feelings can easily tune in to those of others, which helps them understand where others are coming from and why they are doing or saying certain things. In some professions, it's impossible to do your job well unless you have this skill.

Another reason why people with high emotional intelligence are such valuable team members is that they are good listeners, a trait most people lack. When you listen to someone attentively, you can hear even things that the person cannot or will not say. When you are attuned to someone, you can easily pick up subtle signs of fear, irritation, or anxiety from their body language, facial expression, or the tone of voice, all of which can sometimes be a valuable clue to what the person may be going through.

So, to be sought-after, both as a professional and a friend, you should try and develop skills which will help you cope in the high-tech, high-speed, and high-stress world we live in.

As Amit Ray said in one of his books, "As more and more artificial intelligence is entering into the world, more and more emotional intelligence must enter into leadership."

Chapter 1

What is Emotional Intelligence

Emotional intelligence is about self-awareness, self-management, and relationship management. It's about knowing yourself and being able to manage your emotions, as well as your response to those emotions.

However, although emotional intelligence can be learned, it is not something you learn in a weekend course and be "covered" for the rest of your life. This is a lifelong learning skill, that needs to be practiced and improved on throughout life.

To consider yourself emotionally intelligent, you should try to develop empathy which will make it easy to connect with others and understand how they feel. Empathetic people are those who are genuinely interested in others and who readily offer help and support to those who need it. Not everyone can put themselves in other people shoes and try to understand their motives, which is why empathy is such a valuable skill.

For this very reason, developing emotional intelligence will come easily to someone who is a natural empath or a people person. Others can learn about it in a course or from a book, but as with most other skills, to be good at it, you have to practice and apply emotional intelligence to as many situations as possible.

However, having high empathy is not easy. You have to be willing to tune in to other person's feelings and attitude, to try and understand their behavior, to listen without judgment, etc. Not everyone can do this, which is why many believe that empathy is not a skill, but a natural gift.

In other words, emotionally intelligent people are not empathic only when it suits them, but all the time. This is probably why there are very few highly empathic people around, although it's no secret that empathy can be faked, either to influence someone or for self-promotion.

Although these skills are essential for the workplace, they can also help you improve your relationships outside of work. To develop, and perfect, your emotional intelligence you have to start paying more attention to emotions, yours' and others', begin to listen more and talk less, and try to become more open to other people's point of view.

4 tips on how to develop emotional intelligence:

Get to know yourself
Try to understand why you feel a certain way, and what had triggered such emotions. When you know the triggers, you can either avoid certain situations or, if they are unavoidable, find a way of dealing with them. Understanding triggers help deepen your self-awareness because this helps you

learn how certain situations, emotions or people make you feel, and why. It's very important you learn never to ignore your emotions, even negative ones, but to try and identify them and deal with them.

Try to understand others
Unfortunately, most of us are usually too busy to care. Life has become very complicated and competitive, as a result of which, just keeping your head above water is a challenge, let alone sharing what little spare time or energy you have with others.

Besides, in the Western culture, as well as in societies where there is a high turnover of staff and people constantly move around, regularly changing jobs and cities they live in, most of the relationships are superficial and based on interest. To understand somebody else's motives and emotions, you have to be willing to devote your undivided attention and mind to that person. You have to really want to understand their behavior and attitude, to listen attentively for hours if you have to, to be happy for them, or be sad with them.

This can be particularly hard if you are dealing with someone who is full of long-held anger or frustration. So, although empathy can be developed with perseverance and good listening skills, those who are naturally caring and compassionate are the most empathetic.

Think before you speak
Once you identify your emotion and know what had triggered it, take some time to understand it and "process" it, before responding to it. In other words, let it sink in before you react. If overwhelmed with emotions, it may help to ask yourself why you feel the way you do. When you know why something had made you feel angry, embarrassed or betrayed, it becomes much easier deciding what your next step should be.

Learn about the importance of self-management

If you learn how to identify, control, and express your emotions, you will know how to use them in a way that's most effective under the circumstances. Many people underestimate the importance of expressing their emotions in a mature way. Just like ignoring or repressing emotions is bad for your health, so is overreacting, ie expressing emotions without any consideration for how they may affect others.

Therefore, keep on reminding yourself that although held-back emotions create tension, both internally and externally, those expressed in a rush and without thinking are like shooting without aiming. The best way to improve your self-management is to have more emotional self-control and constantly work on enhancing your integrity.

Chapter 2

The Benefits of Emotional Intelligence

Emotional intelligence is believed to be one of the fastest growing job skills, and for a reason. Those with high emotional intelligence have an advantage over others in the workplace mainly because they cope better under pressure, find it easier to work in multicultural environments, and being good listeners, make emphatic colleagues and potentially great leaders.

Therefore, developing emotional intelligence makes it easier to cope with the demands of a stressful and fast-paced life of the 21st century. This is particularly important for those who see themselves in high-paid, prestigious, or leadership positions.

Therefore, the main benefit of having high emotional intelligence is that knowing how to effectively manage emotions, and being able to easily understand and cooperate with others, you stand to be an asset to whomever you work for.

Besides, emotionally intelligent people process their emotions before responding to them. In other words, they think before they speak. This may not seem very important but chances are if you have a habit of making ill-informed comments, you will sooner or later come to regret them.

This is perhaps particularly relevant for the Western culture where people usually don't like silence and tend to answer questions or make comments without thinking. Or even worse, believe that every silence has to be filled with a witty comment or a remark.

Words can both help and hurt, and your choice of words says a lot about you. So, one of the ways of raising your emotional intelligence is to become more conscious of the implications of what you are saying.

What makes people talk without thinking?

On the one hand, information overload has made us overstimulated and we find it more and more difficult to stop the inner chatter. On the other, prolonged silence easily opens the door to feelings we may be trying to keep buried, eg emptiness, hurt, frustration, etc.

However, if on the other end of the scale you have an emotionally intelligent person who can manage their emotions and use words appropriately, it's no wonder they are so often headhunted by the most reputable companies.

10 main benefits of having high emotional intelligence:

People enjoy working with/for you

Emotionally intelligent people don't harass their staff or bully their colleagues. They know how to get others to do what they want without resolving to arrogance or aggression. Being flexible and open to suggestion, they make great colleagues or leaders.

People easily open up to you
Being empathic, emotionally intelligent people can tune in to others' emotions, so they easily understand others' point of view or the circumstances which may have led them to do certain things.

You are a master of your emotions in any situation
The ability to identify, understand, and manage your emotions means you'll always be a step ahead over others when it comes to responding to challenging situations. Besides, being in charge of your emotions helps you manage stress better.

You easily resolve conflicts

The trick to successfully resolving conflicts is to deal with them before the situation gets out of hand. Your ability to manage your emotions, and easily understand those of others, as well as triggers that may have led to them, makes it possible to respond to someone's behavior in a way that will diffuse a potentially difficult situation.

Because your interpersonal skills are good, you feel relaxed around people and are not easily thrown off balance in unpredictable and difficult situations, or with unfriendly or openly hostile individuals.

You easily become a leader
Emotionally intelligent people have most of the traits of highly effective leaders: they are empathic, confident, communicative, positive, and supportive.

You can work anywhere, with anyone
Great people skills, empathy, and social awareness mean that you will be able to work well and get

most out of every situation even under challenging circumstances or in a foreign culture.

You easily get a high-paid job
Being one of the most sought-after skills in the workplace, high emotional intelligence can help you get the job of your dreams.

You don't do or say things you later regret
Knowing that you have to understand and process your emotions before releasing them, means that you will only act once you've had a chance to consider the situation. Sometimes, all it takes is having a few minutes to think things over and give yourself a chance to calm down and assess the situation, before making the final decision.

If there are occasions that you are too embarrassed to think about because of what you said, or did, it's probably because at the time you didn't have or didn't use your emotional intelligence, as a result of which you made decisions you lived to regret.

You are a valued friend and confidant
Emotional intelligence skills are just as valuable outside work, as some of your most important decisions and emotions take place outside the workplace, eg with your family, in your romantic relationships, with your friends, children, etc.

You are fulfilled
Having a successful career and being accomplished personally means you will have lived your life to the fullest.

So, through affecting your emotions, behavior, and interpersonal relations, emotional intelligence has a major effect on the quality of your life.

To continually cultivate and enhance these skills, you should never stop working on your:

Self-awareness
Be constantly in touch with your feelings and learn to tune in to them.

Social skills

Cultivate your communication skills and never underestimate the power of words. Besides, to become highly empathic, you have to try and develop humility. Although being humble is not easy in a society which encourages competition and individuality, ability to openly admit your limitations and mistakes, are traits of a true leader.

Emotional regulation

Learn to control your strong emotions, particularly negative ones, and never act on impulse. Practice this by thinking of something that will make you feel hurt, angry, or exploited. Sit with the feeling, feel the humiliation, or anger, "digest" it, and only after you have calmed down "respond" to the person or situation that made you feel that way.

Chapter 3

Raising Your Emotional Intelligence

Emotional intelligence is something you need to work on throughout life. There are professions, or lifestyles, where high emotional intelligence may not be that necessary, however, most of us could do with better people skills, both in and outside work.

There are many ways of developing or enhancing your emotional intelligence. However, whichever method you decide to use, your efforts should focus on the seven simple routines which will help raise your EQ and indirectly make it easier to reach your goals, whatever they may be.

7 ways to raise your emotional intelligence:

Develop self-awareness

Self-awareness is about self-knowledge, about being mindful of what is happening in your life, and about having a plan how you see your career or life developing. To be self-aware you need a certain level of maturity and at least a vague idea of what you'd like to do with your life. When you know what you want, it becomes easier to find a way of getting it. If you don't, you are left drifting aimlessly, with neither a goal nor a plan.

So, how do you develop self-awareness? Start by increasing your sensitivity to your own emotions and gut feelings, as they are usually the most trusted friends you'll ever have. Try to set aside some time for self-reflection, and reflect on your behavior, thoughts, feelings, frustrations, goals, etc.

Those who are used to self-analysis will probably find this easy, but if you are not used to this kind of thinking, this may be hard, even unsettling. In that case, start by setting aside 30 minutes every evening, once you're done with the work for the day and can relax a bit, and reflect on the day or week behind you. If you had a particularly difficult day/week, ask yourself what you can learn from the experience.

The purpose of this exercise is to get you used to thinking about how you feel and why.

Or, you may start journaling, and this is not about keeping a diary and covering your day-to-day activities and thoughts. Journaling is about writing down any unusual or frustrating experiences, thoughts or emotions you may have had. Some things are not easy to discuss with others, and anyway, not everything is for sharing, so why not get it off your chest by writing about it. The best thing about journaling is that to write something down, you have to think about what to write, and it is often this process of thinking about a problem that helps you see what is at the root of it. So, if feeling upset, disappointed or angry, write it out and move on.

Understand your emotions and what triggers them

To understand your emotions you have to be willing to feel them. It's sad how many people are afraid of their own feelings, especially negative ones, eg sadness, anger, bitterness, etc and the moment they feel these emotions taking over, they do something that will interrupt their train of thought, eg they may busy themselves with something in order to distract themselves from these unpleasant emotions.

If you recognize yourself in this, you should know that all you will achieve this way is postpone (perhaps indefinitely) facing your own demons and dealing with whatever it is that's troubling you. Emotions need to be experienced and dealt with, not buried.

Emotionally intelligent people are not afraid of their emotions. Whatever it is they feel, they stay with it for as long as it takes for the emotion to be identified. There is a reason you feel the way you do, and instead of ignoring them, you should try to "decipher" your emotions because they are trying to tell you something.

To become good at understanding others, you first have to be able to understand yourself. So, even the emotions you don't really want to feel should be addressed, processed, and let go.

Listen without judging
Good listeners are rare, mainly because this requires a lot of empathy, willingness to give up your time for others, and mental energy to be present while you are listening.

The main trait of a good listener is to listen with empathy, and that means without judging. This is not always easy, and may in some cases be impossible, so if you know you are biased towards someone, it's perhaps better not to talk to them if you know you have already made up your mind about how you feel about what they are going to say.

So, to become a good listener you should try to be

present during the conversation, and stay focused. This may be hard, as some people talk a lot, or have a problem saying what they mean so you may be looking at a couple of hours. However, if you are not really interested in this person, or you are in a hurry, or are not feeling well, try to postpone the conversation for another time. The tell-tale signs of boredom or disinterest, eg glancing at your watch, or checking your cell phone or emails, can be very discouraging and insulting for the person you are having a conversation with.

Emotionally intelligent people show interest in others by encouraging them to speak more (even if they don't agree with what they are saying), and by creating an environment where it's safe to open up and say what you really mean.

So, next time you speak to someone who needs your opinion, advice or simply a shoulder to cry on, try to be patient (some people take a long time to come to the point), focused (set aside this time only for them and switch off your phone), and non-judgemental (give them the benefit of a doubt). By not judging and being open-minded, you may not only help the person by giving them a chance to get something off their chest, but you may also gain insight into what's going on in your team, or a family.

Also, pay attention to body language, both yours' and theirs', eg the tone of voice, facial expression, body posture, etc. To a casual observer, these would be clear signs how both of you feel about the conversation.

Active listening requires a lot of practice, but it is one of those skills that you can practice every day, regardless of where you are, and what it is you are listening to.

Mind-Body Connection

This is about listening to your body and understanding what it's trying to tell you. According to the mind-body connection doctrine, discomfort in a part of your body is a sure sign something is not right. For example, lower back pain is usually linked to financial problems, upper back pain to being overwhelmed with life, a knot in the stomach with fear or nervousness, etc.

Learning to notice these signals and interpret them, can save you a lot of time and trouble when it comes to understanding why you feel a certain way.

But, what often happens is that while your body is telling you that you are nervous, anxious, angry, or hurt, you simply ignore these signs, hoping they would eventually go away.

Unfortunately, Western culture pays too much importance to feeling happy and high all the time, so people are not encouraged to deal with their negative emotions, but are advised to ignore them, eg by repeating positive affirmations, or fix them, by taking something that will make them feel better. Do you really believe that if you ignore your negative feelings, repeat a mantra or take something to make you feel high, you will eventually become happy, confident, and fearless???

Sometimes, when you're overwhelmed with emotions, it may be OK to calm yourself down, even in unhealthy ways, until you can think clearly. But, this only offers temporary relief and is not a solution to your problem.

Emotional intelligence can help you get to the bottom of your emotions by showing you how to work out what the triggers are, and how to interpret and release these emotions in the least harmful way.

Engage
How involved are you with your community? Do you volunteer? Is there someone you are regularly helping with by moral support, financially or otherwise? Are you there for others if they need you even if you know it will ruin your weekend which you had planned to spend with your family?

Empathy is the main trait of emotionally intelligent people, and it can easily be developed by anyone if they follow a few simple tips on how to develop or improve these skills. But, the best way to develop empathy is through practicing it. In other words, whenever you engage with others, you are doing what emotionally intelligent people do: you listen, you try to understand, you tune in.

However, many people fake empathy simply because they'd like to be seen as emotionally intelligent. They say the right thing, are always politically correct, appear to be full of deep empathy, listen carefully, offer help, etc. However, if caught off-guard or if for some reason not feeling in the mood for putting up an act, their true nature quickly comes out. Today, to advance professionally, especially if you see yourself as a leader, you have to prove that you have high emotional intelligence, so those who fake it usually do that for self-promotion.

The easiest way to increase your empathy is to start taking interest in others, eg how they live, what's troubling them, how they cope, etc. Improve your listening skills and try to have at least one deep conversation a month. By engaging with others, you automatically raise your emotional intelligence.

Develop self-management
Self-management is about controlling your emotions, not in the sense that you suppress them or ignore them, but learn to deal with them, and only release them after you have understood and processed them. Self-management is also about being true to yourself. Some of the ways you can improve your self-management are through developing your integrity, eg:

- Practice what you preach
- Be prepared to speak up, even if you risk being made fun of
- Don't make promises you are unlikely to keep
- Always be polite and respectful with colleagues,

regardless of how close you may be
- Be self-disciplined, especially if you expect that of others

Learn to deal with criticism

Negative feedback is often undeserved and a result of the person giving it is not fully aware of your performance, or perhaps using the opportunity to sabotage your self-confidence, or openly undermine your career.

However, if truth be told, in every negative feedback there is usually a grain of truth. Although there may have been very good reasons why you underperformed or had a score of people complain about you, the fact is you failed. However, when you come to a stage when you can accept negative feedback, or open criticism, without taking it personally you demonstrate that you have both self-confidence and emotional intelligence.

So, how to become more open to negative feedback? First of all, not all criticism is equally important, nor should you react to it in the same way. A colleague's remark about your new hairstyle could be a sign she's making fun of you, but it could also be a subtle suggestion that the style doesn't suit you.

Besides, if you repeatedly receive less than satisfactory feedback on your performance, or behavior, instead of sulking or throwing a tantrum, try to look at yourself through other people's eye. What if you really ARE lazy, or short-tempered, or unreliable?

The key thing is to ask yourself why you feel bad about the feedback. Is it because it's really undeserved and a result of the person giving it not having a full picture, or are you angry with yourself for not having masked your underperformance better? Or simply jealous others did better?

Admitting you were wrong is not easy, but living in denial is even worse. So, rather than feel upset about the feedback, try to learn something from it.

Especially if it's not the first time the same thing had been brought to your attention.

But, regardless of how you feel, bear in mind that negative feedback, if given without malice, can do more for your personal development, than can false praise.

Besides, there is something noble about admitting you were wrong. It may not be a pleasant thing to do, but it shows you are mature enough to take both the credit for your successes and blame for your mistakes. This may encourage others to do the same.

Closure

The world is changing faster than anyone could have imagined and what has changed dramatically in the last fifty years, is the workplace. There are many social, political and economic reasons for this, but the bottom line is the modern world requires skills that were not only unnecessary a few decades ago, but may not even have existed. So, as the world evolves, so the workforce has to keep up – the introduction of new technologies, new ways of working, emphasis on cultural sensitivity, etc.

The reason emotional intelligence has become one of the most sought after skills in the workplace, is that it revolves around the qualities essential to being successful in the modern world: empathy and ability to work in the culturally diverse environment, ability to work under pressure, willingness to embrace change, strong interpersonal skills, etc.

However, emotional intelligence is even more important for your personal relationships. When you improve your communication skills and empathy, you become more confident, more understanding, and more tolerant. As a result, you are popular because people find they can trust you and don't mind opening up to you.

When you are an active and empathic listener, you easily understand your partner's needs and feelings. And, knowing how to resolve conflicts peacefully, you avoid open confrontation which dampens many relationships. As open communication is what keeps a relationship going, you either avoid many relationship problems or skillfully resolve them in a way that doesn't put your relationship, or friendship, in jeopardy.

Besides, as you are more patient with others and more understanding of their emotions, you become better at dealing with your children or aging parents.

So, indirectly, emotional intelligence makes you more popular with friends and colleagues, more lovable to your partner, and more livable, in case you have to share a room or an apartment with someone.

With all this in mind, investing in developing emotional intelligence clearly pays in the long run. Emotionally intelligent people not only cope better with the challenges of the 21st century workplace, but being cooperative, flexible, and adaptable, they stand to succeed in all spheres of life.

So, if you enjoyed this book and believe you could benefit from a more in-depth information on how to develop emotional intelligence and cultivate the so-called critical skills that the workforce of the 21st century is expected to have, you may want to try our **Emotional Intelligence: *The 21-Day Mental Makeover to Master Your Emotions, Improve Your Social Skills, and Achieve Better, Happier Relationship.*** The book offers a glimpse of the essential life skills and teaches you how to communicate effectively and positively.

As Travis Bradberry pointed out, "People who fail to use their emotional intelligence skills are more likely to turn to other, less effective means of managing their mood, and are twice as likely to experience anxiety, depression, substance abuse, and even thoughts of suicide".

Thank you!

Before you go, I just wanted to say thank you for purchasing my book.

You could have picked from dozens of other books on the same topic but you took a chance and chose this one.

So, a HUGE thanks to you for getting this book and for reading all the way to the end.

Now I wanted to ask you for a small favor. **Could you please consider posting a review on the platform? Reviews are one of the easiest ways to support the work of independent authors.**

This feedback will help me continue to write the type of books that will help you get the results you want. So if you enjoyed it, please let me know! (-:

Lastly, don't forget to grab a copy of your Free Bonus book "*Bulletproof Confidence Checklist*". If you want to learn how to overcome shyness and social anxiety and become more confident then this book is for you.

Just go to:

https://theartofmastery.com/confidence/

www.ingramcontent.com/pod-product-compliance
Lightning Source LLC
Chambersburg PA
CBHW060034040426
42333CB00042B/2440